The Insider's Guide to...
GOOD
MEDICAL CARE

Lindiwe F. Greenwood, M.D., FAAFP

$\mathscr{T}$he Insider's Guide to... GOOD MEDICAL CARE

By Lindiwe F. Greenwood, M.D., FAAFP

Contact: theinsidersguide@yahoo.com

Website: www.doctorgreenwood.com

Library of Congress Cataloging-in-Publication Data
Greenwood, Lindiwe F.

The Insider's Guide to... GOOD MEDICAL CARE

p cm.
ISBN-13: 978-1456377113

ISBN-10: 1456377116

First Paperback Edition

TABLE OF CONTENTS

The Insider's Guide to...
GOOD MEDICAL CARE

Introduction 1

The Major Players in Medicine 3
 Training Lingo 3
 Types of Doctors 4
 Specialties 6

Understanding How Docs Become Docs 13
 Behind the Scenes in the Medical World 14
 Understanding Various Health Care Settings 15
 Understanding Insurance 19
 What to Expect: The First Visit 21
 Understanding "The Rules" 24

Continuing Education for Your Good Medical Care 29

Additional Resources and Information 31
 Top 10 Things Your Primary Care Doctor
 Wished You Knew But Never Told You 31
 Preventive Medicine: What to Discuss With Your Doctor......35

Board of Medical Specialties 39

$\mathcal{T}$he Insider's Guide to...
GOOD MEDICAL CARE

$\mathcal{I}$ntroduction

If you are reading this, it means you took the first step in finding a more effective, thorough and better-informed way to handle your health care. Over the next several pages, I will walk you through the basics of good health care, as well as behind-the-scenes, insider information to help you make the best choices for your medical care. You might be wondering why I am qualified to sell this information. The truth is I'm not only a patient, but I am also a Board Certified Physician, and I have had the dubious honor of looking at health care from both sides of the fence.

I was inspired to write this book after having so many friends, family members, and patients bombard me with questions over the years. It's not that I mind explaining things. After all, that is what I do for a living.

However, it *did* concern me that something as important as health care and its players were so elusive and confusing for the average person. Also concerning is the fact that the information isn't often available to those who want it. If there is info out there, it is typically one-sided. Through this book, I am going to attempt to fill you in on all the little known facts and "tid-bits" you have always wondered about, but never had that doctor around to tell you.

Sit back and relax with a good cup of caffeine-free coffee ☺! Some of this information will be a review, while other parts will be the latest news; some parts you may even find surprising. It is my hope that after you read this book you will feel better informed and empowered as well as fully- equipped to seek the best health care for you and your loved ones.

The Major Players in Medicine

I think it is best to give a crash-course on "how doctors are made" and also to provide some guidance as to whom you should you go to for what services. You might think that as doctors we would be taught in school the identification of all of the specialties and whom you should see for what. Well, as residency goes along you start to sort of learn these things, but you would be surprised by how much "on the job" training there actually is for doctors. Let's start by taking a look at *doctor lingo 101.*

Training Lingo

▲ **Medical Student:**
Person going to school to become a physician, usually requiring four years of medical school with clinical involvement (patient contact) in years three and four.

▲ **Intern:**
First year resident. During this time the physician often rotates through many different areas of medicine to grasp the full range of the specialty.

▲ **Resident:**
Physician in-training (pays homage to the time when doctors in training literally "lived" at the hospital). This is when a physician gains practical experience and training in their respective speciality.

▲ **Fellow:**
A physician in training who has completed residency but is now completing a specialized fellowship in their specialty of choice. This is called a fellowship; can be 1-4 years.

▲ **Attending:**
Physician who has finished all training and is responsible for overseeing fellows, residents and students, particularly in the hospital.

▲ **Residency:**
Period of three to seven years post-medical school when physicians are trained.

▲ **Fellowship:**
Period in post residency when a physician may undertake further specialized training.

Types of Doctors

▲ **Doctor of Medicine:**
An allopathic doctor, the one who earns an M.D. degree from medical school and represents about 70 percent of all medical school graduates. Many of these doctors study specialties that concentrate on different areas of the body, such as cardiology, gastroenterology and pulmonology.

The Insider's Guide to... GOOD MEDICAL CARE

▲ Doctor of Osteopathy:

Type of medical doctor who attends a medical school and becomes an osteopathic doctor or D.O. These doctors attend an osteopathic medical school (outnumbered by allopathic medical schools by about 12 to 1). Today, there is virtually no difference in the training between the two disciplines, other than a technique called Osteopathic Manipulative Medicine. This technique involves manipulation of the joints and body parts to help in the diagnosis and treatment of injury or disease. Many medical doctors with a D.O. degree go on to general practices in areas like family medicine.

▲ Doctor of Dental Medicine:

Dentists, who attend four years of dental school, and handle the medical care of the teeth and gums. Dentists have a DMD in their titles. There also are doctors who specialize in dental surgery and have a DDS in their titles. Many dentists specialize in areas such as endodontics, orthodontics and pediatric dentistry. Each of these specialties requires additional schooling.

▲ Doctor of Chiropractic:

Doctors, who have a DCM in their titles and attend four years of chiropractic medical college, specializing in joint pain anywhere in the body. Many chiropractic treatments involve the manipulation of the spine; chiropractic doctors work on the principle that misalignments trickle down to affect the nervous system.

▲ Doctor of Optometry:

Doctors attend four years of optometric medical college and have an OD their titles. They are the primary doctors for the diagnosis and treatment of eye diseases and related conditions. An Optometrist is not to be confused with an Opthalmologist, who is an M.D.

▲ **Doctor of Podiatric Medicine:**
Doctor who undergoes four years of podiatric medical college and then a residency program of two to four years. These doctors diagnose and treat diseases and injuries to the lower leg, including the foot and ankle. The degree obtained is a D.P.M.

▲ **Specialist:**
A physician who has completed his or her residency and has also completed a fellowship in a specific area. Once specialists have finished their fellowships, they will offer a specialty, such as surgery or ophthalmology, to patients.

▲ **Sub-Specialist:**
A "specialist within a specialty." For example, a Pediatric Retinal Specialist is in the specialty of pediatrics, ophthalmology, and retinas (part of the eye).

Specialties

The following is a list of most specialties and sub-specialties:

▲ **Allergy and Immunology:**
medical specialty of Allergy and Immunology focuses on the diagnosis and treatment of allergies and some immunological disorders (disorders of the immune system, the system that fights off disease).

▲ **Anesthesiology:**
medical specialty focusing on administering pain-killing drugs during surgery in the operating room. Anesthesiology also

includes the field of Pain Management, a sub-specialty which helps manage chronic (ongoing) pain in patients with prescription medication, injections, or other therapeutic methods.

▲ Dermatology:
Medical specialty focusing on the diagnosis, treatment, and prevention of diseases, disorders, and conditions of the skin. These days, many physicians in this field are also trained in laser and aesthetic practices of skin treatment.

▲ Emergency Medicine:
Emergency Medicine is the field which focuses on emergency or acute medical care of patients who need immediate medical attention due to trauma, accident, or a major medical event. Some of these physicians also practice Urgent Care medicine.

▲ Family Medicine:
A primary care field overseeing the basic healthcare needs and preventive medicine of patients of all ages, from infant to geriatric. Family care is the usually the cornerstone of this practice and often takes place in an ambulatory (outpatient/clinic) setting.

▲ Internal Medicine:
Similar to family medicine in that it includes primary care and basic healthcare management of all areas of a patient's health, internal medicine typically does not include pediatrics or obstetrics like family medicine. Additionally, internal medicine includes more in-depth training and patient care in a hospital setting as well as acute care. Finally, internal medicine includes many more sub-specialties such as:

- **Cardiology** – deals with all things concerning the heart.

- **Endocrinology** – deals with the endocrine system, i.e. diabetes, thyroid, adrenal, etc.

- **Gastroenterology** – deals with the stomach, intestines, rectum, gastrointestinal system, etc.

- **Geriatric Medicine** – deals with healthcare involving those mostly 55 and up.

- **Oncology and Hematology** – deals with cancer and blood disorders, i.e. sickle cell, etc.

- **Hospice and Palliative Medicine** – deals with cancer and any terminal patients in the end stages.

- **Infectious Disease** – deals with infectious disease and its prevention, i.e. TB, HIV, etc.

- **Nephrology** – deals with disease and conditions of the kidneys and dialysis.

- **Pulmonary Disease** – deals with diseases of the lungs and sometimes sleep medicine.

- **Rheumatology** – deals with diseases of the joints as well as autoimmune and connective tissue disease, etc.

▲ **Neurology:**
Medical specialty focusing on the diagnosis, treatment, and prevention of diseases, disorders, and conditions of the brain

and nervous system. Patients who have suffered a stroke, or who battle ailments such as epilepsy, Alzheimer's, or Parkinson's are a few examples of some of the patients who are treated by neurologists.

▲ Neurosurgery:
Surgical specialty of medicine devoted solely to surgery of the brain.

▲ OB/GYN (Obstetrics & Gynecology):
Obstetrics is healthcare for pregnant women, including labor and childbirth and providing a safe delivery of the baby. Gynecology entails the diagnosis, treatment, and prevention of diseases, disorders, and conditions of the female reproductive system. Some physicians choose to practice one without the other. There are also several sub-specialty practices that fall under the larger umbrella of these practices, such as Maternal-Fetal Medicine and Reproductive Endocrinologists, the physicians who deal with female infertility.

▲ Ophthalmology:
Medical specialty focusing on treatment of the eyes and retina. Not to be confused with an optometrist, ophthalmologists can also do eye surgery and prescribe medication unlike optometrists, who typically focus on eyesight correction and screening of eye disease.

▲ Orthopedic Surgery:
Entails surgery of the joints, bones, and muscles. Patients with sports injuries or injuries from an accident may be treated by orthopedic surgeons, as are patients with some types of arthritis in the joints which may be surgically repaired.

▲ **Otolaryngology (E.N.T.):**
Medical specialty commonly known as "E.N.T.," which stands for ear, nose, and throat. Otolaryngology includes office-based care and surgical procedures both in the hospital and in the office. Therefore, a variety of practice environments are available in this field.

▲ **Pathology:**
Medical specialty that deals with tissues and specimens for biopsy to help determine and decipher various disease processes, this includes post-mortem. This physician also supervises and interprets lab data and practices.

▲ **Pediatrics:**
Primary care field of medicine focusing on the healthcare of children, from newborn to age 18 and sometimes 21. Most pediatric jobs are office-based, where routine physicals, immunizations, coughs and colds, and "lumps and bumps" are handled frequently, but also entail handling the newborn nursery at the hospital. However, there are also numerous pediatric jobs available at children's hospitals. There are also pediatric subspecialties such as pediatric surgery and pediatric oncology.

▲ **Psychiatry:**
Entails the treatment of patients' mental health and well-being. Psychiatry may be practiced in an office, providing psychotherapy and medication management for more common psychiatric care, or in a psychiatric hospital for more serious, acute psychiatric issues such as bipolar disorder, schizophrenia, and other issues requiring hospitalization. Psychiatry also involves treatment of patients with addictions, such as drugs or alcohol.

▲ Radiology:
Medical field which entails the use of medical imaging to diagnose a variety of problems across all specialties and body systems. Most all medical specialties work in conjunction with this one for diagnosing and confirming disease processes.

There are also interventionists who have special training in biopsy, vessel ablation, and further specialized interventions.

▲ Surgery:
General surgeons perform a variety of abdominal and laparoscopic surgeries. Surgeons may also sub-specialize to focus on trauma surgery, vascular surgery, plastic surgery, or cardiac surgery, to name a few.

▲ Urology:
Medical specialty involving diagnosis, treatment, and prevention of the urinary tract as well as the male reproductive system. Urology includes office-based care and surgical treatment. If a male is having a problem with infertility, this is the specialty that would deal with this issue as well.

---

*This information was supplemented by information on healthcareers.about.com and a complete list of board recognized medical specialties is listed in table form in the back of this book. *

Understanding How Docs Become Docs

In order to become a doctor, you need to have a four-year undergraduate degree, then a four year medical school degree. After that, things get a little more varied and complex. Once you finish medical school, you are then selected to attend residency. The residency is where a physician in training learns the ins and out of their specialty. The first year is called the intern year.

These terms are remnants from a time when doctors practically lived at the hospital. Residency is anywhere from three years and up to seven years. After the residency, if a physician decides to become a specialist or a sub-specialist, then they will undergo training for an additional one to three years in a Fellowship.

All of this really just points to the fact there are many different types of doctors and the more you know about them and what **YOUR** needs are, the better able you would be to find the right doctor to fit them. As new techniques and even specialties come into existence, this list will get longer. Keeping yourself well-informed and educated about the medical community is the first step to good medical care.

Behind the Scenes
in the Medical World

Now, I just want to take a little time to let you know how this all fits together and how it might affect you if you were in the hospital. So let's say that you have to go into the hospital for a scheduled hernia repair. When you come into the hospital, it would not be unusual for some of your first interview questions (and lets face it, that's what it is: an interview) to be asked by a medical student. This is often the first time a medical student gets to see what patient care and interacting with a real life patient is like. They are often extremely excited and eager to take this task on, and that is a good thing... Many complaints of patients are that as doctors move further up the ladder "no one takes the time to listen." You **WILL NOT** have this problem with a medical student!

The problem is that after about an hour of the student asking you everything from "what is your pets first name," to "what age were you diagnosed with XYZ," that is when the resident is going to come in and ask you all the same things all over again! Now this is not purposeless. Rather, the repeat interview is done for three reasons:

1. It tests the medical student to see if the right questions were asked.

2. It tests you, as the patient, to see if the same answers are given, as sometimes, when our memories are jogged, new facts come to light.

3. The resident's questions are going to be more direct, shorter, and just more generally to the point.

After the resident has asked questions, this is likely the time when the Attending Physician comes in as the "clean up crew" to ask any last remaining questions and to bring it all together. If it is determined that you will need a specialist, the Attending will write a note based on all the other notes to the specialist, highlighting all of the pertinent info. There is a saying amongst doctors: "The higher up you go, the shorter the note and the shorter the questions." All of this is a bit redundant, yes, but it is necessary to ensure that everyone is doing their part, learning and, most of all, that patient-care is at its best.

Just know that each time you answer all of those questions you are doing your part as a patient to help medical education as well as to assist in your own personal medical care. It is also important for you to know that no action or decision done by any part of the medical team (team usually includes the Attending, resident, student, nurse, and social worker) is ever done alone. There are many checks and balances in the system. This is a good thing.

Understanding Various Health Care Settings

Health care is practiced in a variety of different settings. I have discovered over the years that there is always a sub set of people who are disappointed about where and how their care is delivered. I think this is because most patients are not really aware that **WHERE** you go for care is just as important as from **WHOM** you receive care. Below is a short, but not exhaustive, list of the different types of health care settings, as well as what they have to offer, and for whom they might be best.

▲ **Inpatient:**
In the hospital care.

▲ **Outpatient:**
Out of the hospital care; usually office/clinic-based.

▲ **Teaching Hospital:**
Usually a large, often urban or central, medical center with many specialties, physicians, and services. If you are a patient at one of these centers, you will encounter all of the learners that I outlined above. Good for people who want a variety of options, specialties, have difficult or unaccepted insurance, are on a fixed or non-existent income, or are uninsured. Good for anyone who wants a "tried and true" setting, ie Johns Hopkins Hospital, University of Maryland Hospital, UCLA Medical Center, etc.

▲ **Private/Non Teaching Hospital:**
These hospitals tend to be a bit smaller, and you will not encounter all the learners as you would at a teaching hospital, because there are no "home teaching programs." On occasion one of these hospitals will contract with an outside teaching program to have residents visit, but again, there are no residency programs stationed at the actual hospital. Good for anyone who wants a bit less hustle and bustle or anyone who does not want to encounter the "full medical team" as outlined above, but these hospitals still offer many options and specialties.

▲ **VA/Veterans Hospital:**
These hospitals are similar to the ones mentioned above, only their mission is to take care of our country's Veterans. Many of these types of hospitals are "self contained" and offer all types of services to those who qualify as Veterans and their family members.

▲ **Community Hospital:**
A smaller hospital, usually only staffed and run by community doctors, some may be on staff, while others may be affiliated only. There are most likely no teaching programs or learners. Good for someone who wants a smaller, more personalized hospital experience.

▲ **Federally Qualified Health Center:**
These are community health care centers that take care of patients in an outpatient setting (meaning not in the hospital). Their mission is to care for all patients, regardless of income or insurance status. These centers are subsidized or given money by the government to be able to offset the cost of caring for those who cannot pay the full fees. There is also a "sliding fee scale" set up at these centers so that a patient is able to pay based on income ability. The center will also have associated services such as social work, sometimes dentistry, etc, to offer to the patients. Good for the patient who may have financial challenges, but still wants quality care. This is also a good hospital for the patient who wants all of the services under "one roof." The challenge is that sometimes there can be a long waiting list to get in to see a physician.

▲ **Multispecialty Group Practice:**
This is a private practice group offering many different specialties all under one roof. For example, under one entity you can find OB/GYN, Internal Medicine, Cardiology, Pediatrics, family medicine, etc. These groups can contain anywhere from two to 20+ physicians. Good for outpatient care that is more "one stop shopping." This scenario is also good for people who have insurance that most groups accept. People who desire a variety of physicians to choose from and who prefer a larger setting for their healthcare outside of the hospital prefer these practices.

▲ **Single Specialty Group Practice:**

This is a private practice group offering many physicians practicing the same type of physician services. This is good for patients who would like a variety of physicians to choose from. This type of practice is also ideal for the patient who does not want to wait to see a specific doctor and can see other doctors from the group when the doctor is out of town or sick

▲ **Solo Practice:**

This is a private practice group offering one physician who delivers all of the health care services at the practice. This is ideal for people who prefer a smaller, more intimate setting, with more personalized care. This setting is also good for people who want to ensure that they see the same physician each time.

Please note that the list above is not exhaustive and many of the settings discussed may be varied and differ from location to location, and state to state. There may also be practices that have a combination of the above, for instance, many hospitals have federally-qualified health centers associated and/or attached to them. There could also be a solo practitioner office that is attached to a hospital.

These notes were meant to be a very general guideline to better help you decipher the best place for you and your family to seek medical care and attention. In reality, many patients are not given a choice where they can seek medical care, due to emergency, location, or convenience.

Understanding Insurance

It is no secret that insurance is a long term investment that has a lot of controversy and complexities surrounding it. For the scope of this book, I will just touch on the most common different types of insurance that exist.

▲ **HMO:**

Standing for Home Maintenance Organization, HMO is considered the most restrictive type of insurance, but is often the least expensive. The pros of HMOs are that they may be a good insurance for you if you tend to have a large number of yearly physician visits. There is usually a relatively small co-pay, and as long as there is "permission" or a referral from your primary care physician, most all services are covered. The drawback is being required to get a referral to see specialists. Additionally, once you have selected a primary care physician, this physician's name must be on the card for proper billing. This type of plan encourages the patient to stay within network for all medical care.

▲ **PPO:**

Standing for Preferred Provider Organization, PPOs are less restrictive than HMOs and, hence, are often more expensive. In this type of insurance organization, permission is not required to seek physician services for doctors or specialists outside of the network. However, there is often an out-of-pocket deductible that must be met before the patient will have all services covered. The benefits of this type of plan include flexibility and the inclusion of a prescription plan all within a large network of physicians.

▲ POS:

Standing for Point Of Service, a POS plan is a hybrid of the above two mentioned plans (HMOs and PPOs). There is often more flexibility than there is with an HMO plan, but not as much flexibility as the PPO plan. The advantage of being able to see out-of-network physicians is there, however, it comes at the price of you having to fill out additional paperwork in order to be reimbursed for the additional fees for out-of-network providers. This reimbursement is often at a lower price than what is paid by the plan member. If the care is kept in-network, then fees are all around less expensive.

▲ EPO:

Standing for Exclusive Provider Organization, the EPO system is very similar to the HMO in that the primary care physician is the main orchestrator of medical care. However, given that patients must stay in-network, the lower or "bulk pricing" for services is negotiated by the company with the physicians, so in-network care is encouraged, and providers are only paid for services provided.

▲ High deductible Plan:

This type of plan, as the name suggests, has a large deductible, however, once you sign up for this type of plan, you are often eligible for a Health Savings Account (HSA). This money can be used tax-free to pay for out–of-network providers as well as for a flexible and varied amount of health care services such as acupuncture and massage therapy. In this plan, you pay a great deal up front, but once you meet your deductible, your out-of-pocket expenses are minimal.

▲ Fee for Service:

The physician requests a particular price, and this is what he or she receives without any issues other than cost to the patient.

This is paid up front and at the time of service. Many practitioners are happy to provide you with the necessary paperwork to get reimbursed. However, these services are not billed through insurance; it is the patient's responsibility to seek reimbursement through the insurance.

What to Expect: The First Visit

Once you have determined where you are going to go for health care, it is important to be armed with information as well as questions to ask your doctor, so that there is an increased chance your expectations will be met at your first visit and subsequent visits. At the back of this book, there is an article I wrote regarding the "Top 10" things you wish you knew about medical care. One of these things is that a great deal of information is asked from you at your first visit. It is best if you come to your appointment prepared with all of the information necessary to answer these questions.

An example of the information I request from my patients is listed below. These may vary from physician to physician, but are typically used across the board.

▶ **Basic information** such as name, address and social security number.

▶ **All insurance information** – you should have a copy of the actual card (it is very important to know your basic benefits and eligibility.)

▶ **Drug/food/environmental allergies** and the reactions that follow when exposed.

▶ **Immunization status**, particularly documentation as to whether you have had your childhood shots, the date of your last tetanus shot, and if you have had a pneumonia shot if over age 65. Furthermore, you should note if you have ever had a reaction to any of these immunizations in the past.

▶ **Full Family history** – especially, but not limited to, cancers, diabetes(sugar), hypertension (high blood pressure), seizure disorders, birth defects, and high cholesterol. It is very important to know the age of diagnosis for any family member diagnosed with breast cancer or colon cancer, because you and your family members will need to be screened at least ten years prior to the age your relative was when the cancer was diagnosed.

▶ **Your Past Medical History** – I cannot tell you how many times patients initially will say they have no medical history, only to find out later they have been diagnosed with high cholesterol, had open heart surgery, and had seizures ten years ago. It's as if since they are relatively healthy now, they do not think it is necessary to mention. In the medical world, nearly all information related to health is relevant and worth mentioning, especially on the first visit. The other thing to note is that once you have been diagnosed with a chronic illness, such as depression, you will, for the most part, always carry that as part of your past medical history. It might be controlled off-meds or in remission, but the tendency and, therefore, the diagnosis is still there and valid.

▶ **Current medications** – It is very important for you to bring your medications in with you to your first visit. A change in just one or two letters can mean the difference between bladder medication and a pain medication. It is great to know your medications, but if you bring them in the physician will be able to go over each one and get ALL the correct information for your records and theirs. I often have my patients type their list of meds if it is lengthy. This way, they can carry it with them on their person when needed for accurate recall.

▶ **Your Questions or Concerns** – Typically, a doctor will ask if you have any questions. But on the spot, most people can't think of anything or have so many questions that they cannot remember them all. Prepare for the appointment by jotting down a few questions, so that you can remember when the time comes. Try also to keep in mind that if things go as they should, this will not be your **ONLY** opportunity to ask questions and meet with the doctor. Sometimes patients try to get through two hours worth of material in only 30 minutes only to cite that "I just have sooo much to ask and want to make sure I get it all in." Well, this makes sense in thought, but in reality, it's just not usually practical to go over two hours worth of questions and information with a doctor who has other patients to see. But you can be prepared and keep it as concise and organized as possible, understanding that an open and ongoing dialogue with your physician should be both welcome and encouraged. Be aware that your doctor may prioritize the issues and have you come back to discuss some specific issues exclusively. Providing the new physician with your old records can help a great deal, while most physicians will not go through records "on the spot." The records help the physician to get acclimated with your past medical history, visits, allergies, etc. If you sign a release, then in some cases it is easier for the physician's office to request the records for you.

All in all, the first visit should give you a good idea of the physician's personal and office style. If you are uncomfortable in any way, this is the time to look elsewhere for a doctor better suited to your personality and needs. Likewise, if you are getting a great vibe and you feel "at home" then nine times out of ten, you will feel comfortable there in the future.

Understanding
"The Rules"

You may be wondering what I mean by "the rules." This is just a term I choose to use to describe some of the insider knowledge that may help you to get more out of your patient/doctor relationship. These "rules" by no means are exhaustive or necessarily even transferrable from one doctor to another. Quite frankly, you could even say that much of what I am about to share is my opinion. However, I truly believe that just by opening up a dialogue regarding these things, you can maximize what you gain from each doctor's visit.

I learned very early on that the patient's agenda and the doctor's agenda is not necessarily the same. If you can even remember just a few of these six "rules" from the list below about communicating with doctors, I promise your physician will thank you and the doctor-patient relationship will benefit.

1. **Try not to "pile on" medical complaints.** This not only is frustrating for the physician, but it also results in a less-than-optimal encounter for the patient. If the doctor's schedule reads "headaches" and you come in wanting to discuss an ingrown toenail, hemorrhoids, and a need for ten of your

meds to be refilled and reviewed, the physician's thoughts become fragmented because there was likely not enough time allotted for these discussions. Due to this unexpected change in the appointment, the chance that something will not be addressed to your satisfaction has increased exponentially. While it may seem efficient and reasonable to the patient to ask questions when they have the doctor's attention, the doctor's have a different perspective. It's much like if you were at work and plugging away on one project, and your boss walks up and dumps five more projects on your desk. Doctor's ideally prefer one to two issues per visit. Often, the doctors will need more time to appropriately diagnose and treat all problems, so if you have more than two, make an additional appointment and specify your expectations.

2. **Please show up at least 15 minutes early to your first appointment.** Yes you may have to wait, but this will give you time to get to know the front desk staff and they can get to know you. If you have logistical questions, this is a good time to ask, and any paperwork that needs to be filled out can be completed without a rush.

3. **If you have been waiting for over 30 minutes and someone has not told you that you are coming up next or offered you an explanation of why there is a delay, please alert the front desk.** I cannot tell you how many times I have experienced this personally or have had patients experience being inadvertently left off the list, waiting for some awful amount of time, yet no one at the front desk was aware. Don't assume. If it is taking too long, without good reason, then you should inquire. You will

likely find, that the doctor is often in the back asking, "Is my 2 o'clock here yet?"

4. **Lateness is not always the fault of the doctor.** All it takes is for one patient to be 5 minutes late, then it is, excuse the expression, "all down hill from there." If everyone over the course of the day is just 5 minutes late (Let's face it, this is probable and logical), after ten patients, the doctor is now running 50 minutes late! I am sorry if you are the one patient who was not late, but is still seen late. Of course, this is not fair, but just give it some consideration before you determine that your doctor should be labeled late or inconsiderate. Most doctors can make-up time in other visits, to get caught back up, especially if the patients are armed with the knowledge found in this book, particularly "Rules" 1, 2, and 3.

5. **No one likes forms, including the doctor!** For most of us doctors, paperwork is a thorn in our sides, just as much as it is to you. Multiply one form by 15-20 patients per day, and...well, you get the idea! Especially during busy times like back-to-school the paperwork can really pile-up for doctors. To help ensure your personal deadlines, school deadlines, etc., are met, please present forms 7-10 days before they are due. Also, please fill out your part of the form. Lastly, please make sure you are presenting it to the correct physician. Many times I have been given a form that really should go to another physician, such as a specialist. It is also important for you, as the patient, to actually **READ** the form before bringing it in to the physician. I often get forms requiring my signature to show I have reviewed the patient's input, or there are labs that need to be obtained to go along with the form,

like in the case of a school physical form. I am always surprised when patients are unaware of these requirements because they never really looked at the form before handing it over to me.

6. **Use good communication.** If at anytime you are not happy with your physician's services or are struggling to understand the doctor's directions, please contact them by phone or e-mail or make an appointment as soon as possible. It is also beneficial to understand any labs that are being ordered, medication changes, and side effects, as well as interim patient tasks and or responsibilities. For most physicians, "no news is good news." Therefore, if we do not hear from you, we are assuming that the prescription, modality, specialist, etc., has worked out fine and you are on your way to recovery. Clear communication from all parties is key to a good health care relationship.

Continuing Education for Your Good Medical Care

The Insider's Guide to Good Medical Care is just a few pages of information to help you on your way to establishing and maintaining a good and fulfilling relationship between you and your medical professional. In the next pages, you will find a few more resources and articles to further address some of the topics we've discussed. This is Book One in a series of mini-books on different facets of health care from an insider's point-of-view.

This book and its series are not intended to take the place of discussion with your personal physician, prescribed medical advice, or good old-fashioned common sense. Please check soon for forthcoming titles in the series. You may also go onto our website, **www.doctorgreenwood.com**, and post any suggestions or requests for mini-book topics.

Additional Resources and Information

Top 10 Things Your Primary Care Doctor Wished You Knew But Never Told You

When I first thought to write this article, I have to be honest, my thought was that people might not understand or be open to the sentiment. However, upon second thought, I think it's time the lines of communication between doctor and patients be opened. It is my hope to communicate to the "masses" some basic but very important sentiments that I would venture to say at least 80% of physicians think, but never express. *Here we go:*

10. **The average doctor does not own stock in pharmaceutical companies.** Therefore, if a medication is prescribed, it is more often done with the intent to help the patient. It makes us as physicians look better if we can "fix" the problem without a med, however sometimes a med is needed.

9. **We love to have educated patients.** It used to be that it was a real challenge to try to explain and print out info for

patients regarding a new diagnosis. With the advent of the internet, patients are better informed, armed with questions, and even ready to offer a differential diagnosis. Still, while it is okay to read on the web for background, don't take everything you read as "gospel." There really is no substitute for a good old-fashioned doctor's appointment.

8. Double booking by most doctors' offices is not a desire, but more of a necessity. This practice was born out of the infamous "No Show" rate that is basically anywhere from 10-40% in some practices. In order to survive financially, docs had to fill the space that was created when patients did not call to cancel their appointments. Things come up for all of us, but if you want to cut down on double-booking, then each of us must do our part and cancel our appointments at least 24 hours in advance, so that a new patient may use the slot. A corollary to this is when your doctor is late; it might not necessarily be his or her fault. As a doctor you can be on time and one patient coming late 5 minutes after their appointment will now throw the schedule off. Take this occurrence and multiply x 20 patients a day and now 5 minutes late translates into an hour and a half late. Something to think about!

7. The days of the calling us all GP's are really out dated. Most of us have sat for a grueling and long specialization board test as well as a specified residency (where doctors learn to treat patients in a hospital and clinic setting). This means that there is a very real difference between Family Medicine, Internal Medicine, Pediatrics, and OB/GYN. Take the time to understand the difference. I personally love when my patients care enough to ask me the difference and how they should go about selecting one or all of the above.

6. **It is very difficult to practice telephone medicine.** Imagine you describe what you think are chicken pox to your doctor over the phone and then in reality it is scabies. Well, as you can imagine, this is going to be quite a problem! Also imagine you have a cold that you think might be bacterial, but is really viral, or vice versa and so on and so forth. There really is no substitute for a doctor's visit. On occasion, if you have already been seen, the doctor might at least have a reference exam of which he or she can build upon to try and solve your problem, but in most cases, you should schedule to come in and have an examination.

5. **It is preferred that you take your meds before you come in to be seen.** There is a common misconception out there that when you go to the doctor you should not take your meds because you may have blood work. On the contrary, most of the time, the doctor wants to know what you blood pressure, sugar, thyroid, etc., all look like on your meds. This way, if an adjustment needs to be made, it can be made accurately. If there is a time when you should not take medications, such as before surgery, then your Physician should explicitly notify you of this. Taking your medications before you come in as well as bringing your bottles in for checking and discussion is a welcomed practice. Most doctors do not know what the meds look like and therefore saying "it's the little yellow pill" will not help them remember what you are taking.

4. Information is key to a good first visit. The first visit is extended and takes more time. Most docs will want to know your immunization status, family history, age of diagnosis of family with colon cancer and breast cancer, as well as other bits of information about yourself. A good primary care physician/patient relationship is based upon trust, good communication, sound medical care, and a sense of comfort. I, personally, like to know my patients and understand a bit about their lives, so I can take care of them in a more personalized manner.

3. Make sure you understand your doctor's lingo. A check up, physical, and pap usually mean something different to the patient vs. what they mean to the doctor. You don't want to be disappointed when you schedule what you think is a physical, only to find out you were really scheduled for a follow-up. This is a little thing, but can really put a damper on your satisfaction if not well understood. Feel free to ask questions of your doctor, if you are unsure about the language he or she is using.

2. Everything cannot be fixed with a pill. Sometimes a change in environment, a good book, yoga class, a change in diet, laughter, 8 hours sleep can be just as effective (and safer!).

1. Most patients are not doctors, however, <u>ALL</u> doctors are patients. This means that despite what many people think, most doctors are sympathetic to paying co-pays, buying meds, making appointments and, yes, even having to wait for their physician at their own doctor's appointments. A broken health care system hurts all of us; we are **ALL** in this together!

Preventive Medicine: What to Discuss With Your Doctor

Barely a day goes by that headline news does not feature a story on health care. While many media players focus on health care problems, such as the millions of Americans who are uninsured or the epidemic of obesity, others focus on getting healthier, anti-aging and losing weight.

The up-side to this media coverage is that health is at the top of many people's minds. The downside is that there is so much information, and sometimes conflicting information, that the average consumer doesn't know quite what to do.

With so much to confuse us, the best place to turn is your primary care physician. Even the commercials from manufacturers who have the latest "FDA-approved" remedy finish their sales pitches with a logical call to action: "Ask your doctor."

Your primary care physician is up-to-date on the latest science behind the headlines and commercial claims, and s/he is responsible for recommending the best care for you as an individual, not just one of millions in a set demographic group, such as "menopausal women" or "men over 50."

Make the Appointment:
Be Proactive in Your Health Care

Taking control of your health care begins with one simple action: make an appointment to see your doctor to ensure you are on schedule with your preventive health screenings and tests.

While practitioners are encouraged to follow U.S. Preventive Task Force guidelines and specialty association recommendations, as well as some insurance company suggestions to prescribe tests at specified ages or frequencies, each doctor uses his or her discretion in determining when and how often to recommend a test, based on each patient's unique situation (including lifestyle, family history, symptoms, etc.).

As a general guideline, here are some recommendations for the age to begin certain screening tests or vaccines. Use this as a guide to begin a consumer-informed discussion with your primary care doctor as you commit to your improved health.

For parents with young children, the most important thing you can do is ensure their vaccinations are up-to-date (including tetanus, which should be boosted every 10 years for life). You can also incorporate regular exercise into family time and have their cholesterol checked at least once between the ages of 2 and 18 to get a baseline. If the child eats an unhealthy diet or is overweight, your physician may recommend more regular lipid testing.

Girls/women who are sexually active should have a pap test at least once a year. For those not sexually active, start no later than 21 unless there is a family history of cancer. Also, ask your daughter's doctor his/her opinion of the new HPV vaccine to evaluate the risk of a "new" protocol versus the risk of cervical cancer from the herpes virus.

Teenagers also should be taught how to do monthly breast self-exams or self-testicle exams. Explain to them that any foreign mass should be reported immediately, so a doctor can do further testing for breast or testicular cancer-diseases that affect young and old.

Both teens and adults should have annual complete physical exams. Although it seems the days of the "take all your clothes off" physical is a thing of the past with many primary care physicians, it is important to have your skin examined regularly to detect any new or unusual moles that could indicate skin cancer.

Other Tests and Screenings

Other tests/screenings that should be part of the physical, or performed at least once a year, include:

- ▶ Sexually-transmitted disease screening (after known exposure or relations with multiple partners)

- ▶ Cholesterol testing (under 40: once every five years or sooner if there is a strong family history; age 50 or older: once every one to two years if "normal" and more often if abnormal)

- ▶ PSA test for prostate cancer (for men age 50 and older; age 40 and older for African-American men or high risk population)

- ▶ Digital rectal exam (age 50 and older)

- ▶ Fecal occult exam/colonoscopy (*see below)

- ▶ Mammogram (annual after age 40, or 10 years before the age of diagnosis of breast cancer in an immediate family member)

- ▶ Bone density (routine for 65 years and older, or sooner if there is chronic steroid use, strong family history or high risk factors for osteoporosis)

- ▶ Flu shot (each fall)

A physical should also include a discussion of tobacco, drug and alcohol use and any concerns of depression or other mental health issues. Discussions with your doctor should also address nutrition, sexual practices, advance directives, aspirin use, aging-related body changes, vision and hearing.

*For individuals with a history of colo-rectal cancer in the family, get a colonoscopy 10 years before the age at which your family member was diagnosed and then one every five years. Otherwise, everyone over the age of 50 should have a colonoscopy every 10 years, starting at age 50.

Everyone should get a vaccination for pneumonia at the age of 65, or sooner for those in high-risk groups.

And, on a final note: If you have a family history of anything, or if you're adopted, be extra vigilant. If you have a gut feeling that something may be wrong or a particular symptom is concerning to you, go to your doctor sooner rather than later. Catching a problem early substantially increases the likelihood of successful treatment.

$\mathcal{B}$oard of Medical Specialties

General Certificate(s)	Subspecialty Certificates
American Board of Allergy and Immunology Allergy and Immunology	No Subspecialties
American Board of Anesthesiology Anesthesiology	Critical Care Medicine Hospice and Palliative Medicine Pain Medicine
American Board of Colon and Rectal Surgery Colon and Rectal Surgery	No Subspecialties
American Board of Dermatology Dermatology	Clinical and Laboratory Dermatological Immunology Dermatopathology Pediatric Dermatology
American Board of Emergency Medicine Emergency Medicine	Hospice and Palliative Medicine Medical Toxicology Pediatric Emergency Medicine Sports Medicine Undersea and Hyperbaric Medicine
American Board of Family Medicine Family Medicine	Adolescent Medicine Geriatric Medicine Hospice and Palliative Medicine Sleep Medicine Sports Medicine

GENERAL CERTIFICATE(S)	SUBSPECIALTY CERTIFICATES
American Board of Internal Medicine	
Internal Medicine	Adolescent Medicine
	Advanced Heart Failure and Transplant Cardiology[1]
	Cardiovascular Disease
	Clinical Cardiac Electrophysiology
	Critical Care Medicine
	Endocrinology, Diabetes and Metabolism
	Gastroenterology
	Geriatric Medicine
	Hematology
	Hospice and Palliative Medicine
	Infectious Disease
	Interventional Cardiology
	Medical Oncology
	Nephrology
	Pulmonary Disease
	Rheumatology
	Sleep Medicine
	Sports Medicine
	Transplant Hepatology
American Board of Medical Genetics	
Clinical Biochemical Genetics*	Medical Biochemical Genetics[2]
Clinical Cytogenetics*	Molecular Genetic Pathology
Clinical Genetics (MD)*	
Clinical Molecular Genetics*	
American Board of Neurological Surgery	
Neurological Surgery	No Subspecialties

General Certificate(s)	Subspecialty Certificates
American Board of Nuclear Medicine Nuclear Medicine	No Subspecialties
American Board of Obstetrics and Gynecology Obstetrics and Gynecology	Critical Care Medicine Gynecologic Oncology Hospice and Palliative Medicine Maternal and Fetal Medicine Reproductive Endocrinology/Infertility
American Board of Ophthalmology Ophthalmology	No Subspecialties
American Board of Orthopaedic Surgery Orthopaedic Surgery	Orthopaedic Sports Medicine Surgery of the Hand
American Board of Otolaryngology Otolaryngology	Neurotology Pediatric Otolaryngology Plastic Surgery Within the Head and Neck Sleep Medicine
American Board of Pathology Anatomic Pathology and Clinical Pathology* Pathology – Anatomic* Pathology – Clinical*	Blood Banking/Transfusion Medicine Cytopathology Dermatopathology Neuropathology Pathology – Chemical Pathology – Forensic Pathology – Hematology Pathology – Medical Microbiology Pathology – Molecular Genetic Pathology – Pediatric

General Certificate(s)	Subspecialty Certificates
American Board of Pediatrics Pediatrics	Adolescent Medicine Child Abuse Pediatrics[3] Developmental-Behavioral Pediatrics Hospice and Palliative Medicine Medical Toxicology Neonatal-Perinatal Medicine Neurodevelopmental Disabilities Pediatric Cardiology Pediatric Critical Care Medicine Pediatric Emergency Medicine Pediatric Endocrinology Pediatric Gastroenterology Pediatric Hematology-Oncology Pediatric Infectious Diseases Pediatric Nephrology Pediatric Pulmonology Pediatric Rheumatology Pediatric Transplant Hepatology Sleep Medicine Sports Medicine
American Board of Physical Medicine and Rehabilitation Physical Medicine and Rehabilitation	Hospice and Palliative Medicine Neuromuscular Medicine Pain Medicine Pediatric Rehabilitation Medicine Spinal Cord Injury Medicine Sports Medicine

General Certificate(s)	Subspecialty Certificates
American Board of Plastic Surgery	
Plastic Surgery	Plastic Surgery Within the Head and Neck
	Surgery of the Hand
American Board of Preventive Medicine	
Aerospace Medicine*	Medical Toxicology
Occupational Medicine*	Undersea and Hyperbaric Medicine
Public Health and General Preventive Medicine*	
American Board of Psychiatry and Neurology	
Psychiatry*	Addiction Psychiatry
Neurology*	Child and Adolescent Psychiatry
Neurology with Special Qualification	Clinical Neurophysiology
in Child Neurology*	Forensic Psychiatry
	Geriatric Psychiatry
	Hospice and Palliative Medicine
	Neurodevelopmental Disabilities
	Neuromuscular Medicine
	Pain Medicine
	Psychosomatic Medicine
	Sleep Medicine
	Vascular Neurology
American Board of Radiology	
Diagnostic Radiology*	Hospice and Palliative Medicine
Radiation Oncology*	Neuroradiology
Radiologic Physics*	Nuclear Radiology
	Pediatric Radiology
	Vascular and Interventional Radiology

GENERAL CERTIFICATE(S)	SUBSPECIALTY CERTIFICATES
American Board of Surgery Surgery Vascular Surgery	Hospice and Palliative Medicine Pediatric Surgery Surgery of the Hand Surgical Critical Care
American Board of Thoracic Surgery Thoracic Surgery	Congenital Cardiac Surgery[2]
American Board of Urology Urology	Pediatric Urology

*Specific disciplines within the specialty where certification is offered.

[1] Approved 2008; first issue yet to be determined

[2] Approved 2007; first issue 2009

[3] Approved 2006; first issue November 2009

ABMS Member Boards certify physicians in more than 145 specialties and subspecialties. The preceding chart lists the current specialty and subspecialty certificates offered by ABMS Member Boards.

© 2006-2009 American Board of Medical Specialties. This chart and the contents therein is from the American Board of Medical Specialties website.

Notes

Notes

Notes

Notes

www.ingramcontent.com/pod-product-compliance
Lightning Source LLC
Chambersburg PA
CBHW071254280526
45788CB00004B/1720